# More POP HITS FOR THE TEEN PLAYER

## EASY PIANO ARRANGEMENTS BY DAN COATES

W9-BAE-602

Project Manager: Carol Cuellar
Art Layout: Joe Klucar

DAN COATES® is a registered trademark of Alfred Publishing Co., Inc.

© 2001, 2004 ALFRED PUBLISHING CO., INC.
All Rights Reserved

Any duplication, adaptation or arrangement of the compositions
contained in this collection requires the written consent of the Publisher.
No part of this book may be photocopied or reproduced in any way without permission.
Unauthorized uses are an infringement of the U.S. Copyright Act and are punishable by law.

# CONTENTS

# AMAZED

Words and Music by
MARV GREEN, AIMEE MAYO
and CHRIS LINDSEY
*Arranged by DAN COATES*

Amazed - 5 - 1

© 1999 WARNER-TAMERLANE PUBLISHING CORP., GOLDEN WHEAT MUSIC,
CAREERS-BMG MUSIC PUBLISHING, INC and SONGS OF DREAMWORKS (Admin. by CHERRY RIVER MUSIC CO )
All Rights for GOLDEN WHEAT MUSIC Administered by WARNER-TAMERLANE PUBLISHING CORP.
All Rights Reserved

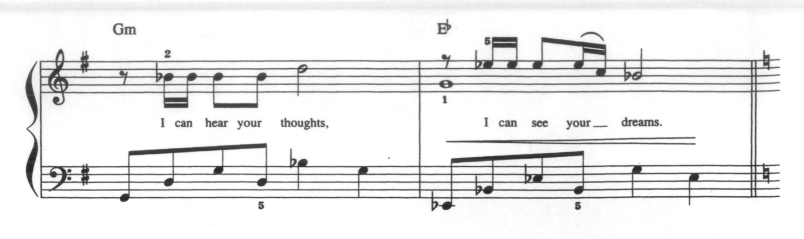

I can hear your thoughts, I can see your__ dreams.

*Chorus:*

I don't know how you do what you do.__ I'm so in love with

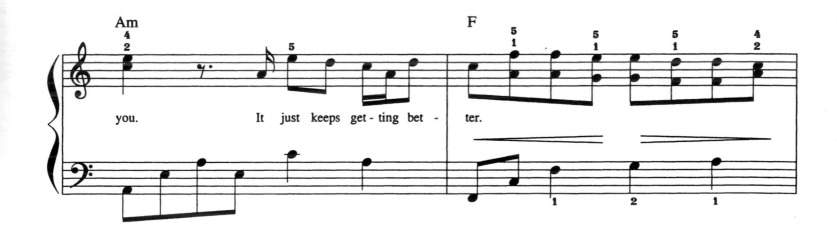

you. It just keeps get - ting bet - ter.

I wan - na spend the rest of my life__ with you by my side__

Ev-'ry lit-tle thing that you do,_____ I'm so in love with

you. It just keeps get-ting bet-ter.

I wan-na spend the rest of my life_____ with you by my side__

for - ev - er and ev - er.        Ev -'ry lit - tle thing that    you

do,      (ev -'ry lit - tle thing     that     you     do...)      ev -'ry  thing   that   you

do,      ba - by, I'm a - mazed    by       you.

*Verse 2:*
The smell of your skin,
The taste of your kiss,
The way you whisper in the dark.
Your hair all around me,
Baby, you surround me.
You touch every place in my heart.
Oh, it feels like the first time every time.
I wanna spend the whole night in your eyes.
*(To Chorus:)*

# BE WITH YOU

Words and Music by
ENRIQUE IGLESIAS,
PAUL BARRY and MARK TAYLOR
*Arranged by DAN COATES*

Moderately, with a steady beat

Mon-day night and I feel so low.___ Count the hours but they

go so slow.___ I know the sound of your voice can

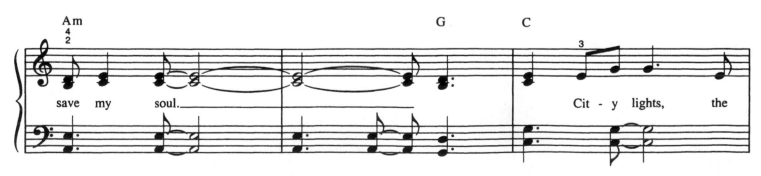

save my soul.___ Cit-y lights, the

Be With You - 4 - 1

© 1999 EMI APRIL MUSIC INC , ENRIQUE IGLESIAS and RIGHT BANK MUSIC
All Rights for ENRIQUE IGLESIAS Controlled and Administered by EMI APRIL MUSIC INC
All Rights Reserved    International Copyright Secured    Used by Permission

streets of gold.___ Look out my win-dow to the world be - low.___

Moves so fast and it feels so cold___ and I'm all a - lone.___ (And I'm

all a - lone.___)

Don't let me die, I'm los - ing my mind.
Don't let me down, come to me now.

I

Ba - by, just give me a sign. } And
got to be with you some - how.

now___ that___ you're

# LIVIN' LA VIDA LOCA

Words and Music by
ROBI ROSA and DESMOND CHILD
*Arranged by DAN COATES*

Fast ♩ = 174

1. She's in - to su - per - sti - tions, black cats and voo - doo dolls. ___

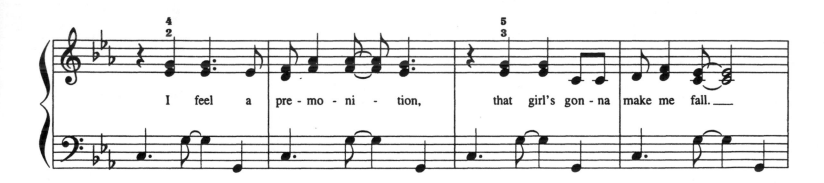

I feel a pre - mo - ni - tion, that girl's gon - na make me fall. ___

© 1999 ARTEMIS MUZIEKUITGEVERIJ B.V., A PHANTOM VOX CORP., DESTON SONGS, LLC and DESMOPHOBIA
All Rights for itself and A PHANTOM VOX CORP. Administered by ARTEMIS MUZIEKUITGEVERIJ B.V.
All Rights for ARTEMIS MUZIEKUITGEVERIJ B.V., DESTON SONGS, LLC and DESMOPHOBIA Administered by WB MUSIC CORP.
All Rights Reserved

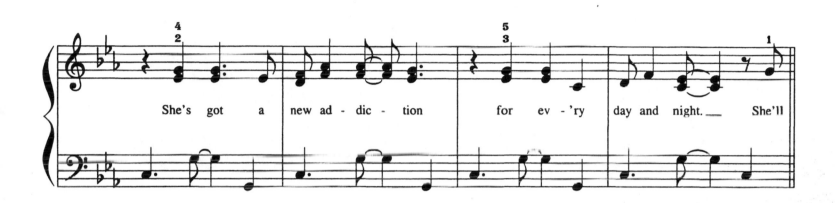

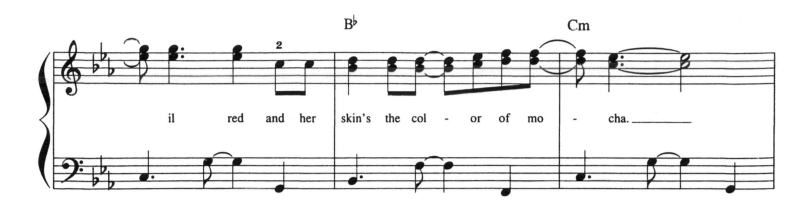

il red and her skin's the col - or of mo - cha.

She will ___ wear ___ you out, liv - in' la vi - da lo -

ca, liv - in' la vi - da lo - ca. She's

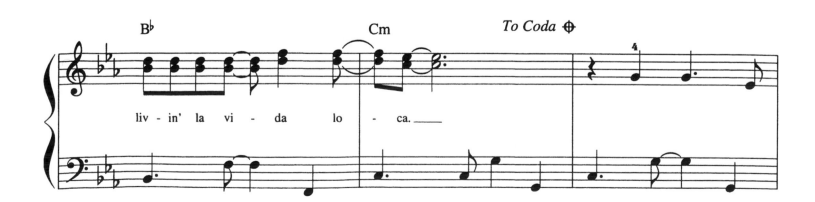

liv - in' la vi - da lo - ca. ___

*To Coda* ⊕

Livin' La Vida Loca - 6 - 4

She will ___ wear ___ you out, liv-in' la vi-da lo-

ca, liv-in' la vi-da lo - ca.

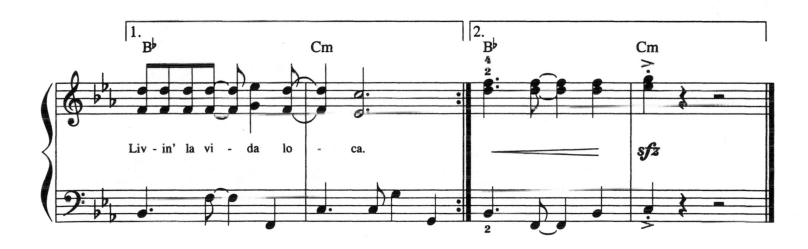

1. Liv-in' la vi-da lo - ca. 2.

*Verse 3:*
Woke up in New York City
In a funky, cheap hotel.
She took my heart and she took my money.
She must have slipped me a sleeping pill.

She never drinks the water
And makes you order French champagne.
Once you've had a taste of her
You'll never be the same.
Yeah, she'll make you go insane.
*(To Chorus:)*

# BYE BYE BYE

Words and Music by
KRISTIAN LUNDIN,
JAKE and ANDREAS CARLSSON
*Arranged by DAN COATES*

**Moderate, steady beat** (♩ = 92)

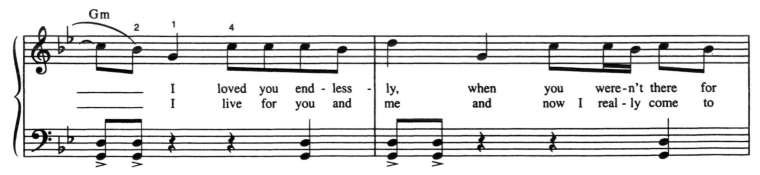

Bye Bye Bye - 4 - 1

© 2000 ZOMBA MUSIC PUBLISHERS LTD (All Rights Administered by ZOMBA ENTERPRISES INC for the U.S.A. and Canada)
All Rights Reserved

### 𝄋 *Chorus:*

20

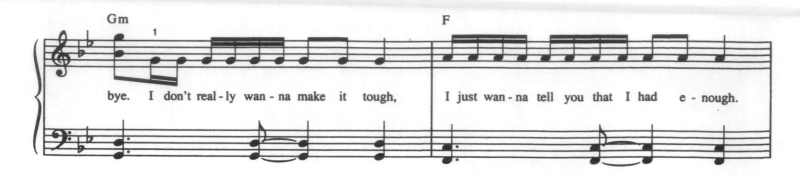

Bye Bye Bye - 4 - 3

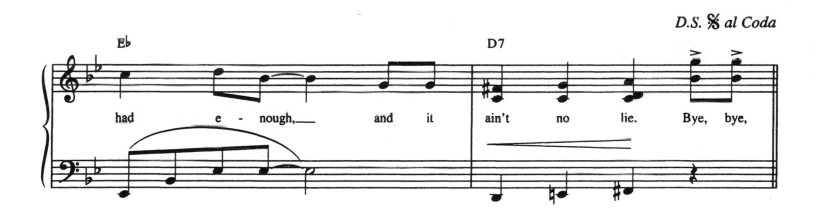

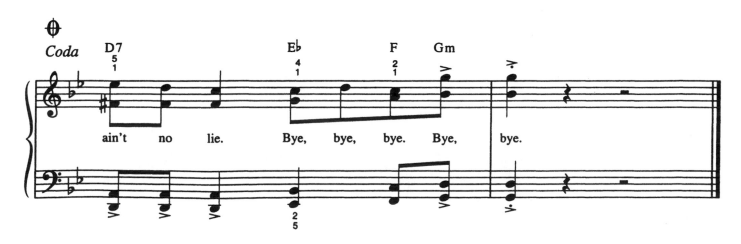

# COME ON OVER
## (ALL I WANT IS YOU)

Words and Music by
PAUL REIN and JOHAN ABERG
*Arranged by DAN COATES*

Moderately fast (♩ = 120)

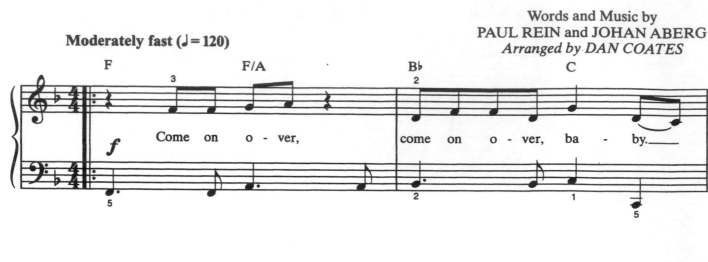

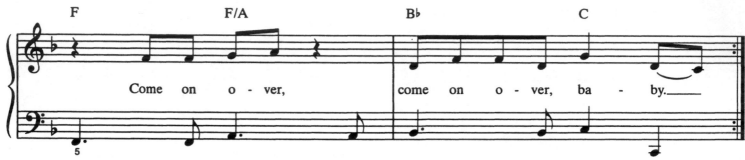

*Verse:*

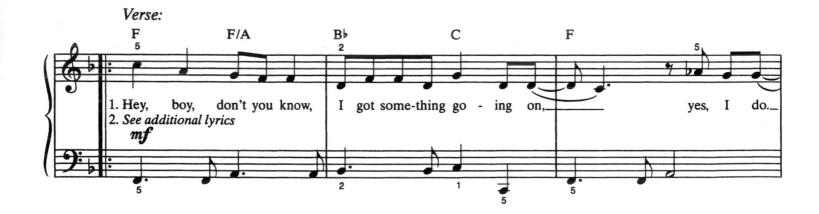

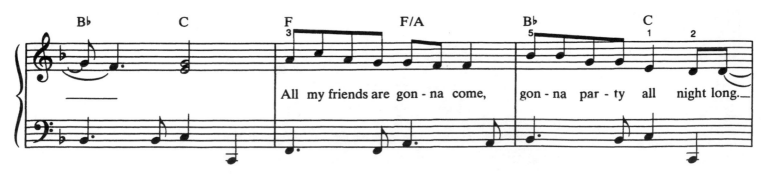

Come on Over - 4 - 1

© 1999 AIR CHRYSALIS SCANDINAVIA AB/ECLECTIC MUSIC/MADHOUSE FORLAG AB/BMG PUBLISHING SCANDINAVIA
All Rights for AIR CHRYSALIS SCANDINAVIA AB in the U.S. and Canada Administered by CHRYSALIS MUSIC (ASCAP)
All Rights Reserved

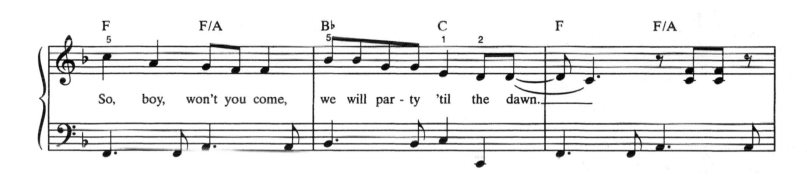

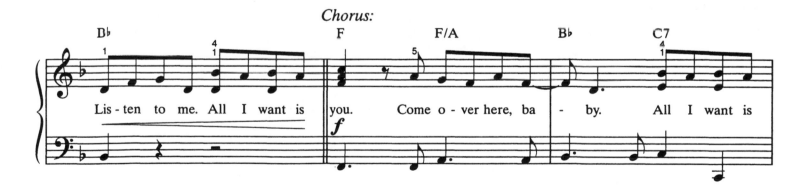

*Chorus:*

you.

All I want is you.

All I want is you. Now, ba - by, don't be shy, you bet - ter cross the line.

I'm gon - na love you right 'cause all I, all I want is all I want is you.

*Verse 2:*
I want you to know,
You could be the one for me, yes, you could.
You've got all I'm looking for,
You've got personality.
I know, you know, I'm gonna give you more.
The things you do,
I've never felt this way before.
So, boy, won't you come,
Won't you come and open my door?
Listen to me.
*(To Chorus:)*

# BEAUTIFUL STRANGER

Words and Music by
**MADONNA CICCONE and WILLIAM ORBIT**
*Arranged by DAN COATES*

Beautiful Stranger - 5 - 1

© 1999 WB MUSIC CORP., WEBO GIRL PUBLISHING, INC. and RONDOR MUSIC (London) LTD. (PRS)
All Rights for WEBO GIRL PUBLISHING, INC. Administered by WB MUSIC CORP.
All Rights for RONDOR MUSIC (London) LTD. (PRS) Administered in the U.S. and Canada by ALMO MUSIC CORP. (ASCAP)
All Rights Reserved

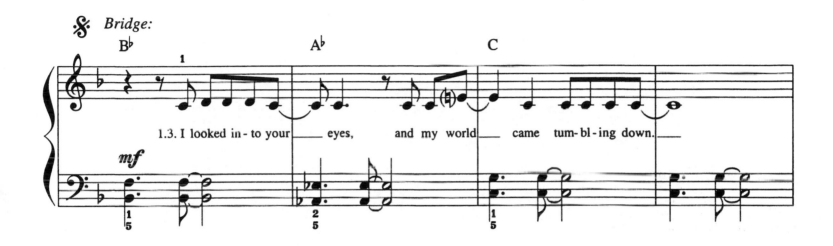

Beautiful Stranger - 5 - 2

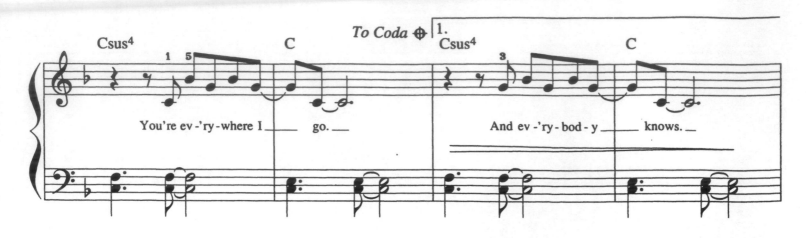

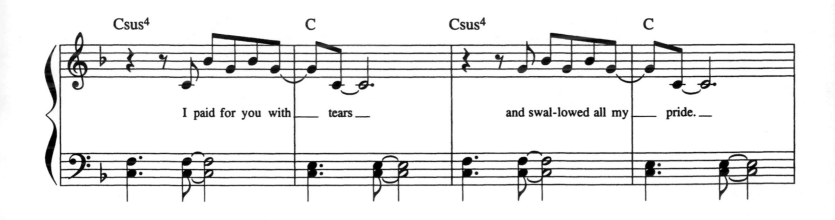

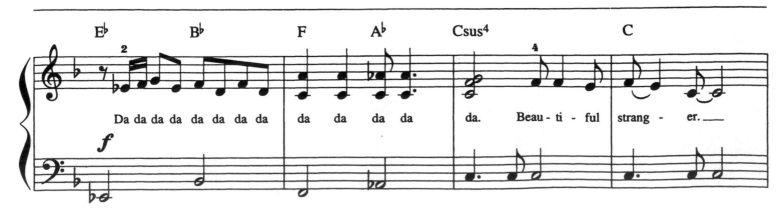

Da da da da da da da da da   da   da   da   da.   Beau - ti - ful   strang - er. ___

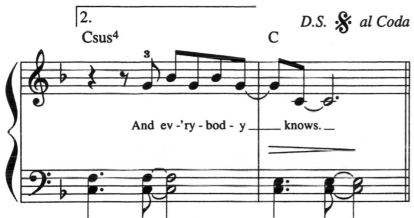

2.

**D.S.** 𝄋 *al Coda*   *Coda*

And ev -'ry - bod - y ___ knows. ___   And ev -'ry - bod - y ___

___ knows. ___   I paid for you with ___ tears ___   and swal - lowed all my ___

___ pride. ___   Da da da da da da da da   da   da   da   da

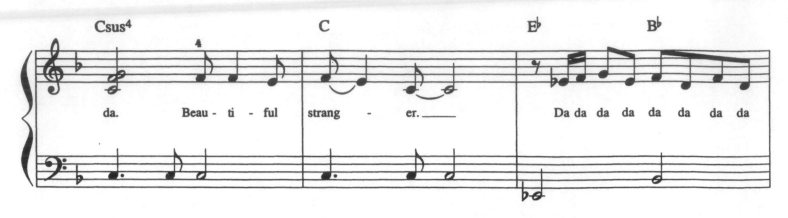

*Verse 3:*
If I'm smart, then I'll run away.
But I'm not, so I guess I'll stay.
Haven't you heard?
I fell in love with a beautiful stranger.

*Bridge 2:*
I looked into your face,
My heart was dancin' all over the place.
I'd like to change my point of view,
If I could just forget about you.
*(To Chorus:)*

# GIVE ME JUST ONE NIGHT
## (UNA NOCHE)

Words and Music by
CLAUDIA OGALDE, ANDERS BAGGE
and ARNTHOR BIRGISSON
*Arranged by DAN COATES*

Moderately fast (♩ = 124)

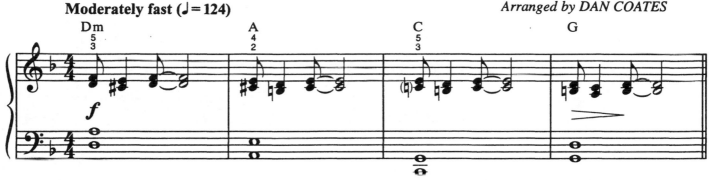

**Verse 1:**

1. Your lips keep tell-ing me you want me,_____ and hold me close all through the

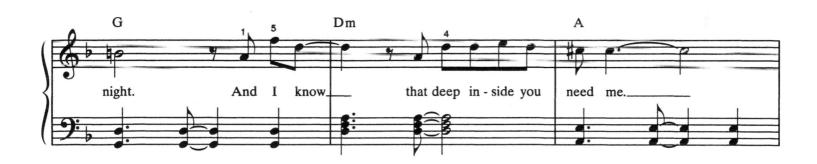

night. And I know____ that deep in-side you need me.____

**Verses 2 & 3:**

No one else can make it right.

2. Don't you try to hide your
3. Your eyes with pas-sion make me

Give Me Just One Night - 3 - 1

© 2000 Air Chrysalis Scandinavian (ASCAP), Murlyn Songs AB/Universal Music Publishing Ltd. and Murlyn Songs AB/EMI April Music Inc.
All Rights for Air Chrysalis Scandinavian Administered in the U.S. and Canada by Chrysalis Music
All Rights for Universal Music Publishing Ltd. Controlled and Administered in the U.S. and Canada by Universal - PolyGram International Publishing, Inc.
All Rights Reserved

I'll give you the time of your life.

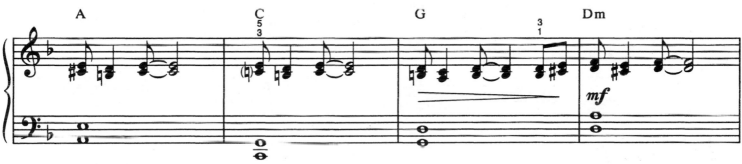

Give me just one

# I STILL BELIEVE

Words and Music by
ANTONINA ARMATO and
BEPPE CANTORELLI
*Arranged by DAN COATES*

I Still Believe - 4 - 1

© 1987 CHRYSALIS MUSIC, TOM STURGESS MUSIC and COLGEMS-EMI MUSIC PUBLISHING
All Rights for TOM STURGESS MUSIC Administered by CHRYSALIS MUSIC
All Rights Reserved

# GRADUATION
## (Friends Forever)

Words and Music by
COLLEEN FITZPATRICK
and JOSH DEUTSCH
*Arranged by DAN COATES*

**Moderately slow (♩ = 160)**

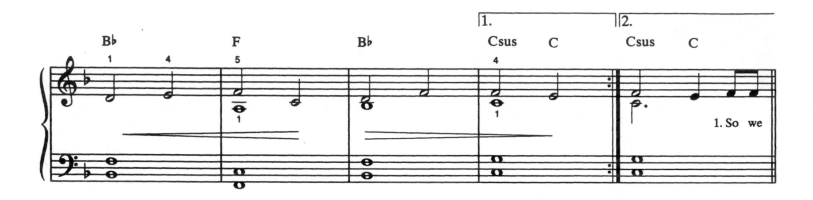

*Verse:*

talked all night a-bout the rest of our lives,___ where we're gon-na be when we turn___

___ twen-ty-five.___ I keep think-ing times will nev-er change,___

Graduation - 5 - 1

© 1999 WARNER-TAMERLANE PUBLISHING CORP., BLANC E MUSIC and BIG BLACK JACKET MUSIC
All Rights Administered by WARNER-TAMERLANE PUBLISHING CORP.
All Rights Reserved

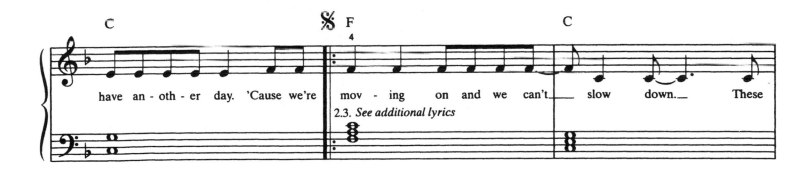

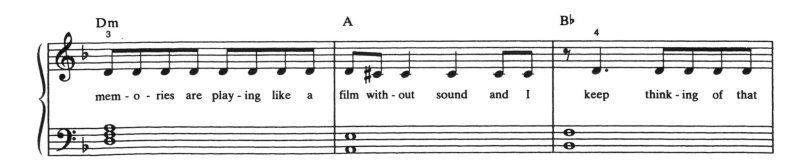

Graduation - 5 - 4

come what - ev - er, we will still be friends for - ev - er.

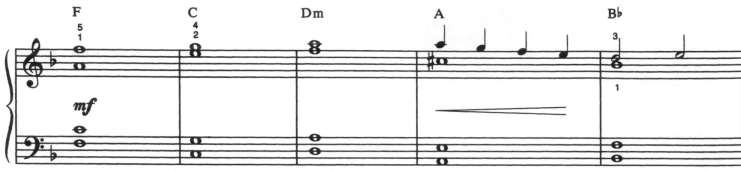

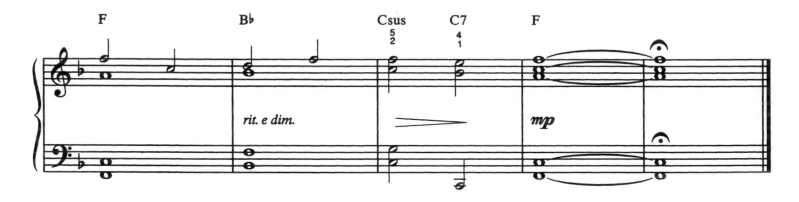

*Verse 2:*
So if we get the big jobs and we make the big money,
When we look back at now, will our jokes still be funny?
Will we still remember everything we learned in school,
Still be trying to break every single rule?
Will little brainy Bobby be the stockbroker man?
Can Heather find a job that won't interfere with her tan?
I keep thinking that it's not goodbye,
Keep on thinking it's our time to fly.
*(To Chorus:)*

*Verse 3:*
Will we think about tomorrow like we think about now?
Can we survive it out there, can we make it somehow?
I guess I thought that this would never end,
And suddenly it's like we're women and men.
Will the past be a shadow that will follow us around?
Will the memories fade when I leave this town?
I keep thinking that it's not goodbye,
Keep thinking it's our time to fly.
*(To Chorus:)*

# I TURN TO YOU

Words and Music by
DIANE WARREN
*Arranged by DAN COATES*

I Turn to You - 5 - 1

© 1996, 2000 REALSONGS/WB MUSIC CORP. (ASCAP)
All Rights Reserved

§ *Chorus:*

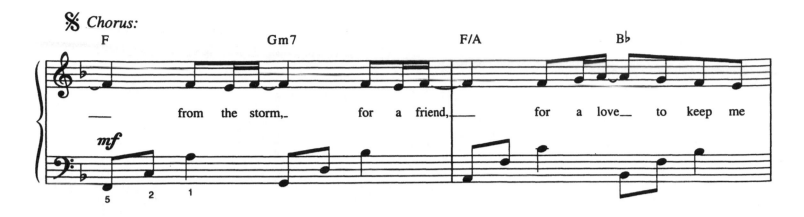

from the storm,_ for a friend,_ for a love_ to keep me

safe and warm, I turn to you._ For the strength_

*To Coda* ⊕

to be strong,_ for the will to car - ry on, for

1.

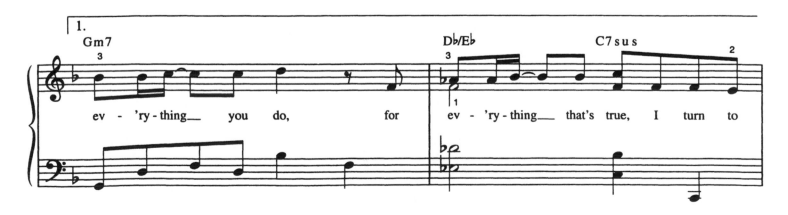

ev - 'ry-thing_ you do, for ev - 'ry-thing_ that's true, I turn to

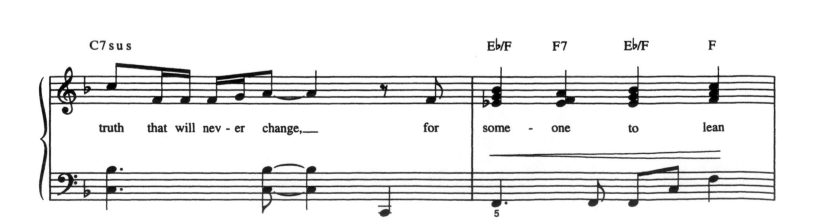

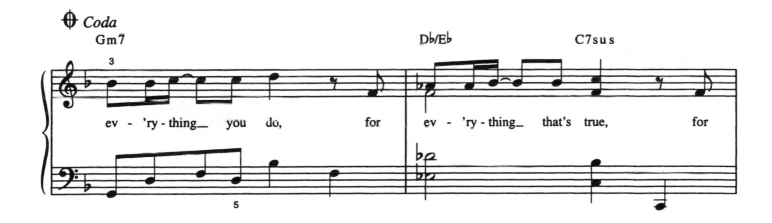

I Turn to You - 5 - 5

# I WANT YOU TO NEED ME

Words and Music by
DIANE WARREN
*Arranged by DAN COATES*

Slowly, in 2 ♩ = 78

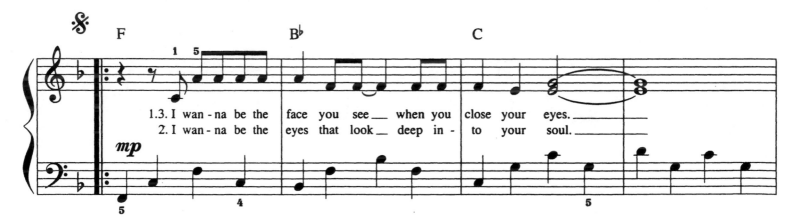

1.3. I wan - na be the face you see__ when you close your eyes.__
2. I wan - na be the eyes that look__ deep in - to your soul.__

I wan - na be the touch you need__ ev - 'ry sin - gle night.__
I wan - na be the world to you.__ I just want it all.__

I Want You to Need Me - 5 - 1

© 1999 REALSONGS (ASCAP)
All Rights Reserved

I wan-na be your fan-ta-sy ___ and be your re - al - i - ty, ___ and
I wan-na be your deep-est kiss, ___ the an-swer to your ev - 'ry wish, ___ and

ev-'ry-thing ___ be - tween. I want you to need me ___ like the
all you ev-er need. I want you to

air you ___ breathe. ___ I want you to feel me ___ in

ev - 'ry - thing. ___ I want you to see me ___ in your

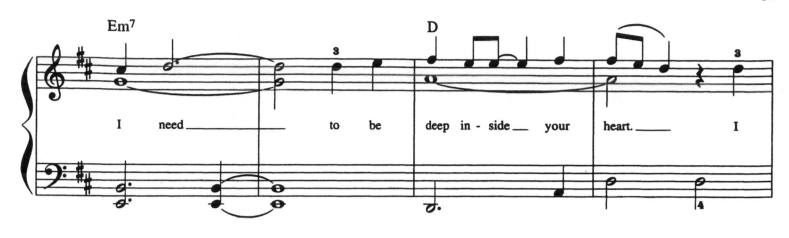

I need _____ to be deep in-side___ your heart.___ I

just want to be ev-'ry-where you are. ___

taste you, feel you, breathe you, need you.___ I want you to

need me _____ like the air you___ breathe.___ I want you to

52

I Want You to Need Me - 5 - 5

# IT'S GONNA BE ME

Words and Music by
MAX MARTIN, RAMI
and ANDREAS CARLSSON
*Arranged by DAN COATES*

It's Gonna Be Me - 5 - 1

© 2000 ZOMBA MUSIC PUBLISHERS LTD
All Rights Administered by ZOMBA ENTERPRISES INC (ASCAP) for the U S A and Canada
All Rights Reserved

*Chorus:*

thing I do nev - er seems e - nough for you. You don't wan - na

lose it___ a - gain, but I'm not___ like them. Ba - by, when you

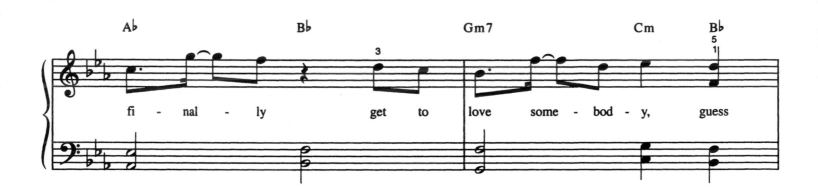

fi - nal - ly get to love some - bod - y, guess

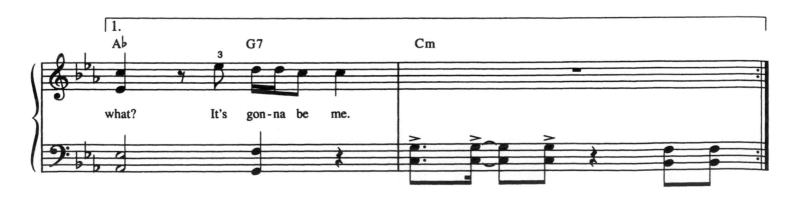

what? It's gon-na be me.

It's Gonna Be Me - 5 - 2

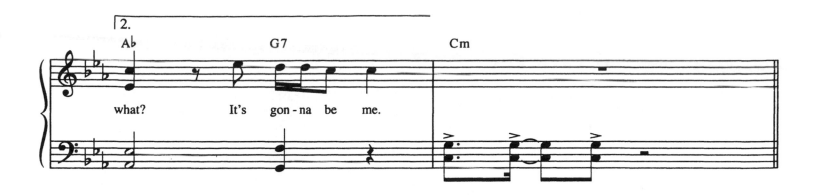

what? It's gon-na be me.

Bridge:

There comes a day when I'll be the one,— you'll see. It's

gon - na, gon - na, gon - na, gon - na,— it's gon-na be me.

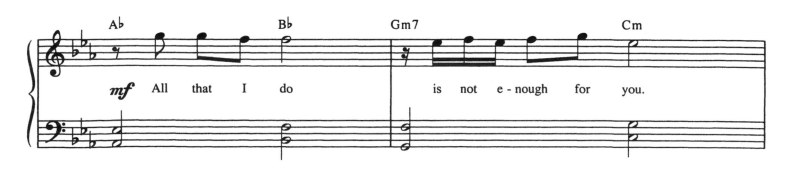

All that I do is not e-nough for you.

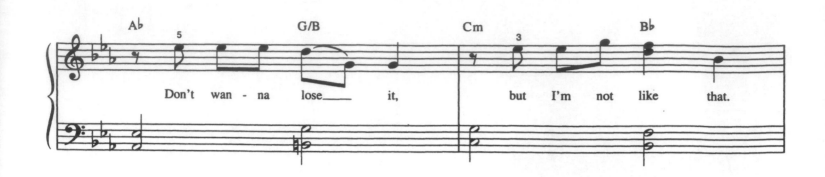

Don't wan - na lose\_\_\_\_ it, but I'm not like that.

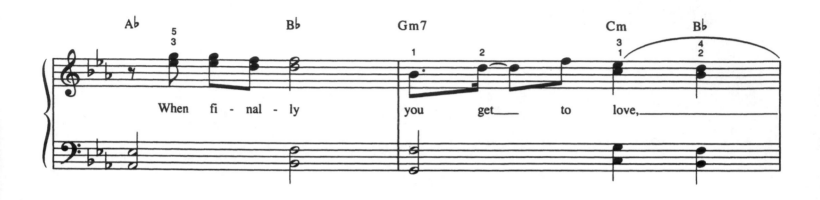

When fi - nal - ly you get\_\_\_ to love,\_\_\_\_

\_ guess what? (Guess what?) Ev - 'ry lit - tle thing I do nev - er seems e -

nough for you. You don't wan - na lose it\_\_\_ a - gain, but

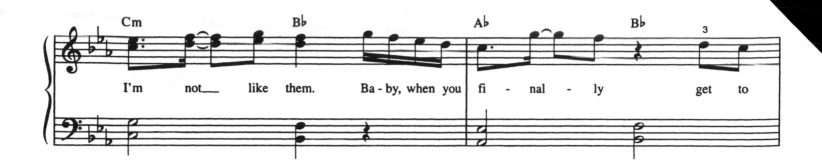

I'm not\_\_\_ like them. Ba - by, when you fi - nal - ly get to

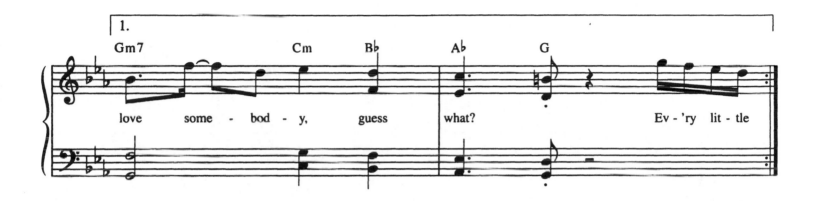

**1.**

love some - bod - y, guess what? Ev - 'ry lit - tle

**2.**

love some - bod - y, guess what? It's gon-na be me.

*sfz*

*Verse 2:*
You've got no choice, babe,
But to move on, you know
There ain't no time to waste,
'Cause you're just too blind to see.
But in the end you know it's gonna be me.
You can't deny,
So just tell me why...
*(To Chorus:)*

# IT'S MY LIFE

Words and Music by
JON BON JOVI, RICHIE SAMBORA
and MAX MARTIN
*Arranged by DAN COATES*

**Steady rock beat (♩ = 120)**

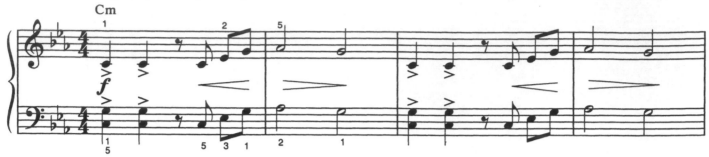

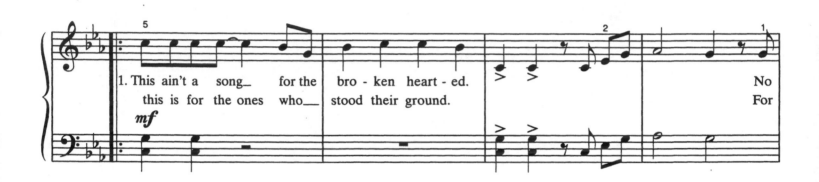

1. This ain't a song___ for the bro - ken heart - ed.
this is for the ones who___ stood their ground.

No
For

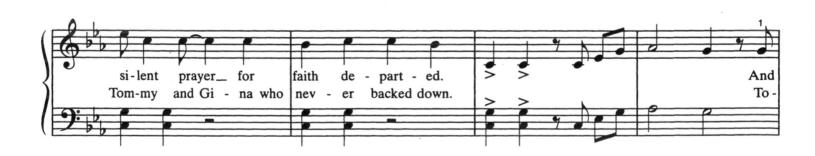

si - lent prayer___ for faith de - part - ed.
Tom - my and Gi - na who nev - er backed down.

And
To -

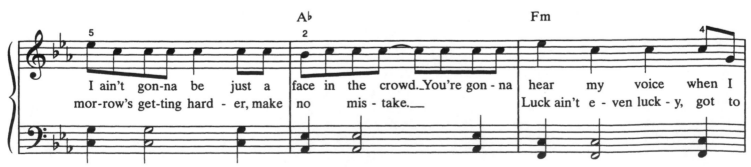

I ain't gon-na be just a face in the crowd..You're gon - na hear my voice when I
mor-row's get-ting hard - er, make no mis - take.___ Luck ain't e - ven luck - y, got to

It's My Life - 4 - 1

© 2000 Universal - PolyGram International Publishing, Inc., Bon Jovi Publishing, Aggressive Music and Grantsville Publishing Ltd.
All Rights for Bon Jovi Publishing and Aggressive Music Controlled and Administered by Universal - PolyGram International Publishing, Inc.
All Rights for Grantsville Publishing Ltd. Administered by Zomba Enterprises Inc. in the U.S. and Canada
All Rights Reserved

shout it out loud.
make your own breaks. } It's my life, it's now___ or nev - er.

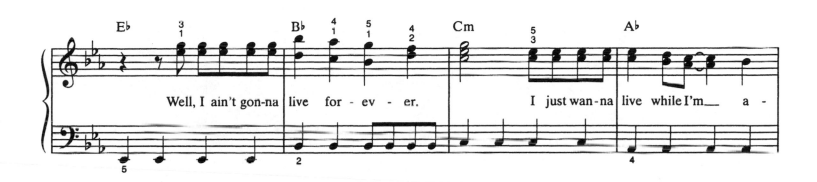

Well, I ain't gon-na live for - ev - er. I just wan-na live while I'm___ a -

live.___ It's my life. My heart is like an o - pen high - way.___

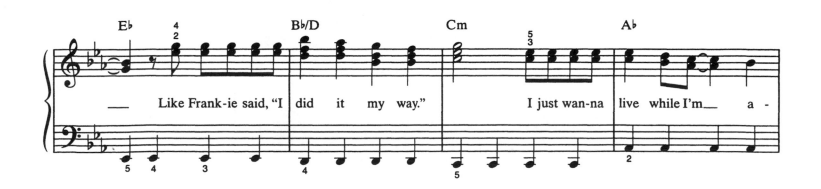

___ Like Frank-ie said, "I did it my way." I just wan-na live while I'm___ a -

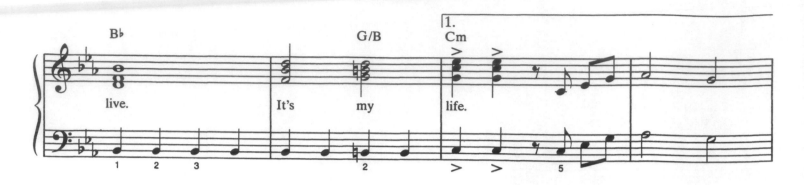

live. It's my life.

2. Yeah, life.

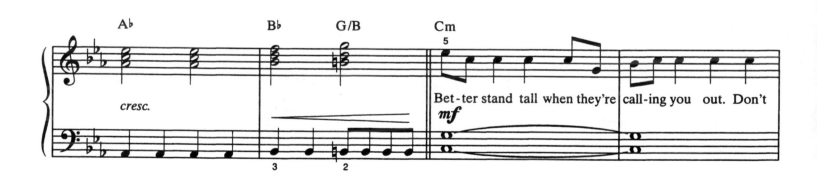

cresc. Bet-ter stand tall when they're call-ing you out. Don't

bend, don't break, ba-by, don't back down. It's my life and it's now

_ or nev - er._ Well, I ain't gon-na live for - ev - er. I just wan-na

live while I'm_ a - live._ It's my life. My heart is like an

o - pen high - way._ Like Frank-ie said, "I did it my way." I just wan-na

live while I'm_ a - live    It's my    It's    my    life.

# LUCKY

Words and Music by
MAX MARTIN, RAMI
and ALEXANDER KRONLUND
*Arranged by DAN COATES*

**Moderate, steady beat (♩ = 96)**

*Verse 1:*

1. Ear - ly morn-ing, she wakes up. Knock, knock, knock on the door.

It's time for make-up, per-fect smile. It's you they're all wait-ing for. They go,

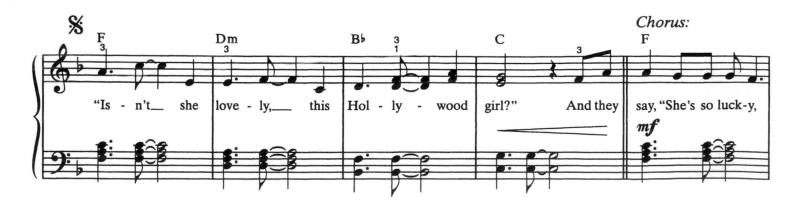

"Is - n't__ she love - ly,__ this Hol - ly - wood girl?" And they say, "She's so luck-y,

*Chorus:*

Lucky - 4 - 1

© 2000 Zomba Music Publishers Ltd./Universal Music Publishing AB
All Rights Reserved

### ⊕ Coda

### Bridge:

"Is - n't\_\_\_ she luck - y,\_\_\_ this Hol - ly - wood

girl?" She is\_\_\_ so luck - y,\_\_\_ but

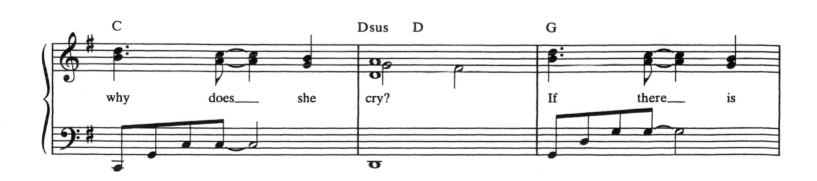

why does\_\_\_ she cry? If there\_\_\_ is

noth - ing___ miss - ing in her life, why do tears come___ at night?

**Chorus:**

*mf* "She's so luck - y, she's a star." But she cry, cry, cries in her

lone - ly___ heart, think - ing, if there's noth - ing miss - ing in my life, then

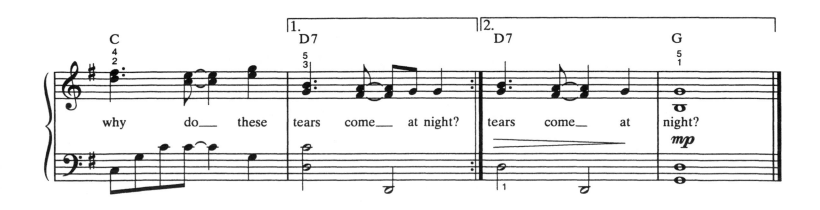

why do___ these tears come___ at night? | tears come___ at night? *mp*

# MY EVERYTHING

Words and Music by
ARNTHOR BIRGISSON, ANDERS SVEN BAGGE,
NICK LACHEY and ANDREW LACHEY
Arranged by DAN COATES

**Slowly, with expression**
*Verse:*

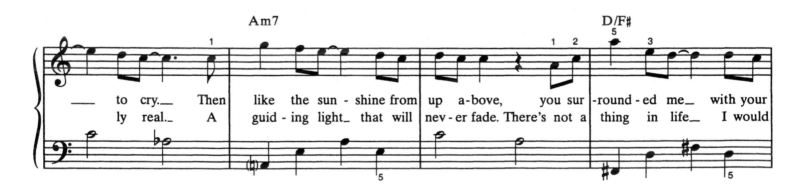

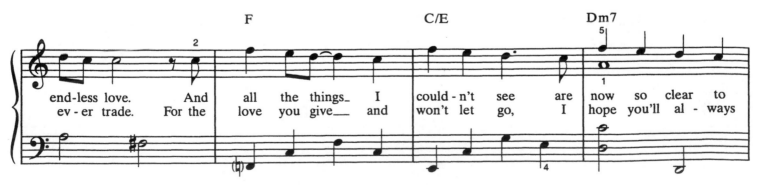

My Everything - 4 - 1

© 2000 Murlyn Songs AB, Air Chrysalis Scandinavia AB and EMI Music Publishing Ltd.
All Rights for Murlyn Songs AB Controlled in the Western Hemisphere by Universal - PolyGram International Publishing, Inc.
All Rights for Air Chrysalis Scandinavia AB Controlled in the U.S. and Canada by Chrysalis Music
All Rights Reserved

*Chorus:*

G7 | C | | Am7

know... } You are my | ev-'ry-thing. | Noth-ing your | love won't bring.

*mf*

F | | | Fm/Ab

My life is | yours a-lone. | The on-ly love I've | ev-er known.

Am | | D7/F#

Your spir-it | pulls me through | when noth-ing | else will do.___

Dm | | Bb

___ Ev-'ry | night I pray___ on | bend-ed knee___ that | you will al-ways

G7 | C | 1. | 2. Cm

be my ev-'ry- | thing. | 2. Now | Oh,___

My Everything - 4 - 2

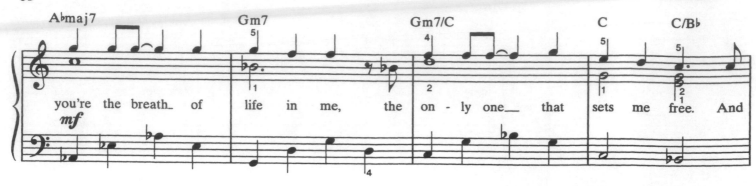

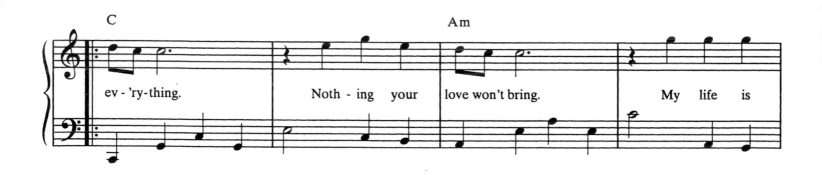

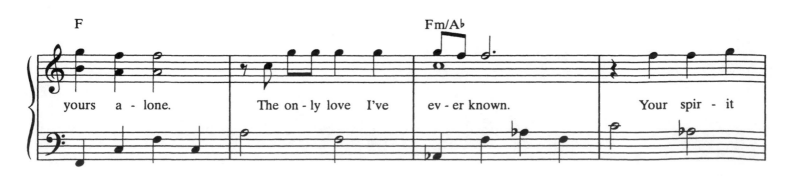

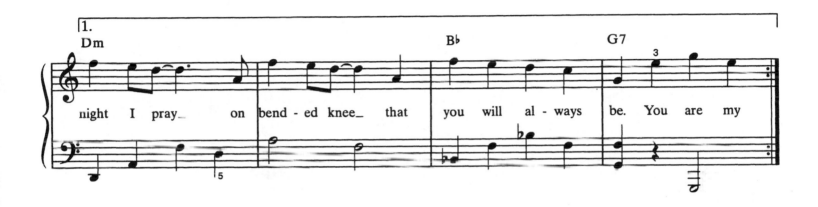

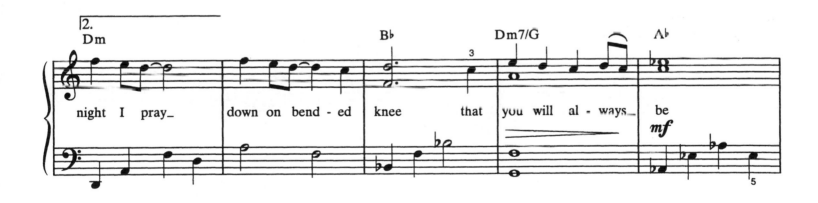

# THE ONE

Words and Music by
MAX MARTIN and BRIAN T. LITTRELL
*Arranged by DAN COATES*

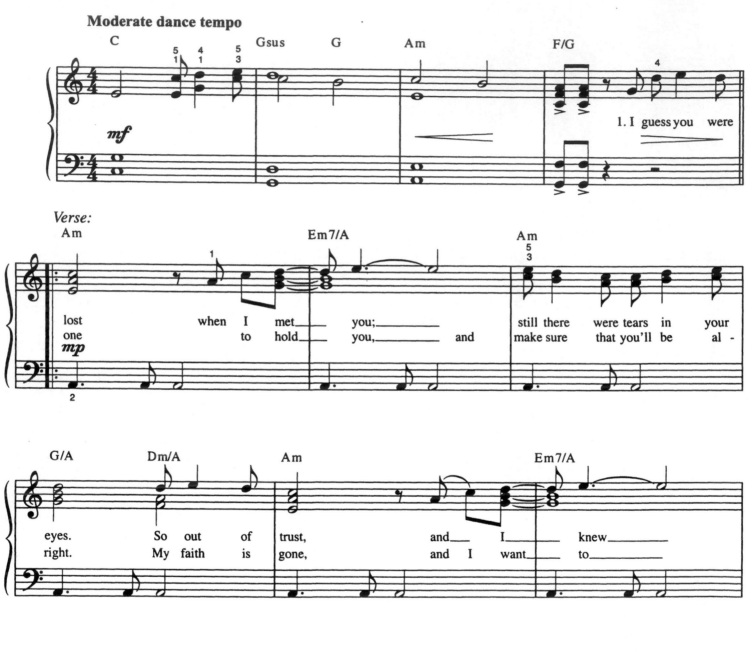

The One - 5 - 1

© 1999 ZOMBA ENTERPRISES INC /B-ROCK PUBLISHING/GRANTSVILLE PUBLISHING LTD
(All Rights on behalf of B-ROCK PUBLISHING Administered by ZOMBA ENTERPRISES INC for the World and
All Rights on behalf of GRANTSVILLE PUBLISHING LTD Administered by ZOMBA ENTERPRISES INC for the U.S.A and Canada)
All Rights Reserved

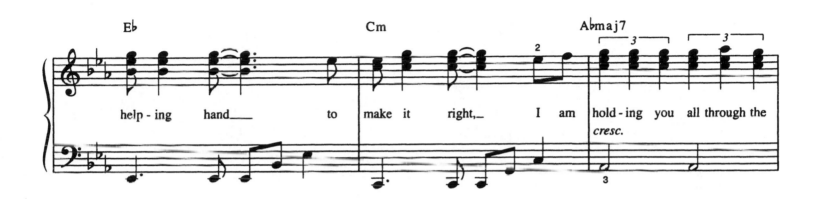

The One - 5 - 2

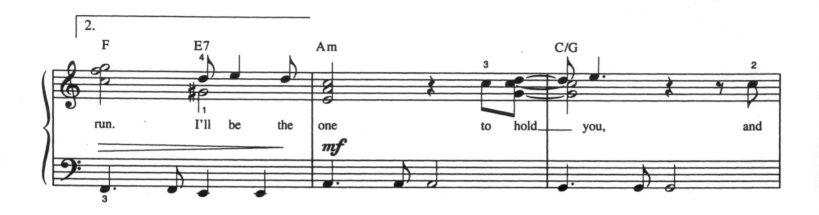

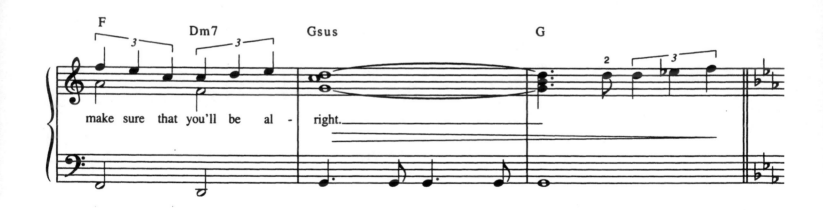

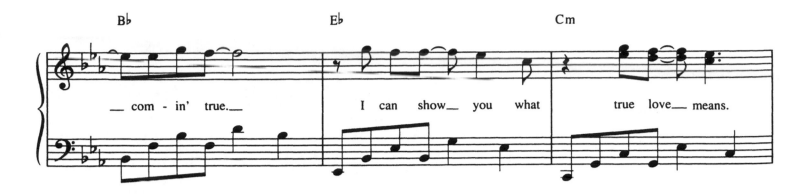

_com - in' true._ I can show_ you what true love_ means.

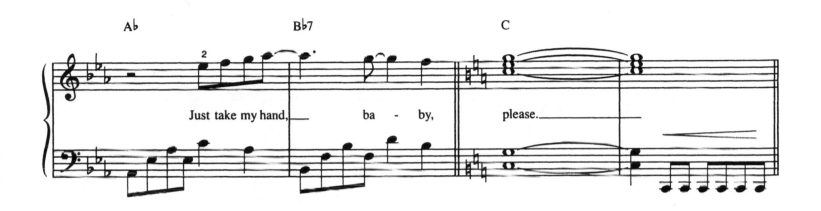

Just take my hand,_ ba - by, please._

**Chorus:**

I'll be_ the one, I'll be _ the_ light where you_ can run

to make_ it al - right. I'll be_ the one, I'll be_ the_ light

The One - 5 - 4

# OOPS!...I DID IT AGAIN

Words and Music by
MAX MARTIN and RAMI
*Arranged by DAN COATES*

**Moderate dance beat (♩ = 94)**

Yeah, yeah, yeah, yeah, yeah, yeah.

1. I think I did it a-gain, I made you be-lieve
2. You see my prob-lem is this, I'm dream-ing a-way,

we're more than just friends. Oh, ba-by,
wish-ing that he-roes, they tru-ly ex-ist.

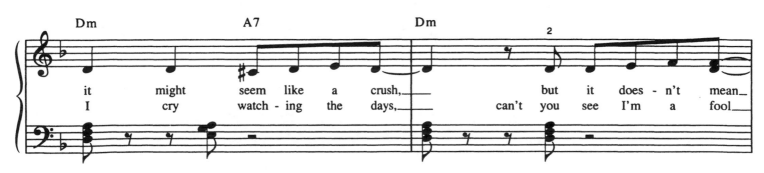

it might seem like a crush, but it does-n't mean
I cry watch-ing the days, can't you see I'm a fool

Oops!. .I Did It Again - 5 - 1

© 2000 ZOMBA MUSIC PUBLISHERS LTD.
All Rights Administered by ZOMBA ENTERPRISES INC. for the U.S.A. and Canada
All Rights Reserved

that I'm se - ri - ous. 'Cause to
in so man - y ways? But to

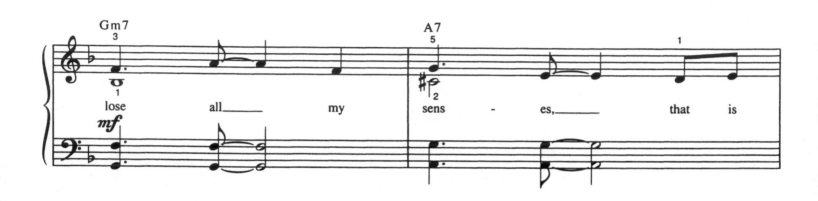

lose all my sens - es, that is

just so typ - i - c'lly me. Oh, ba - by, ba - by.

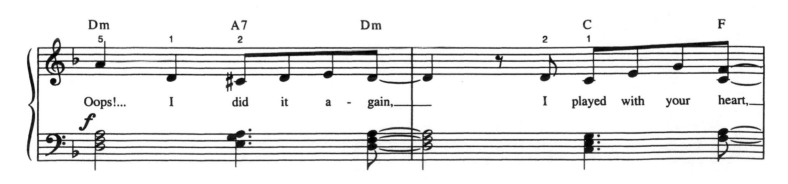

Oops!... I did it a - gain, I played with your heart,

Oops!...I Did It Again - 5 - 2

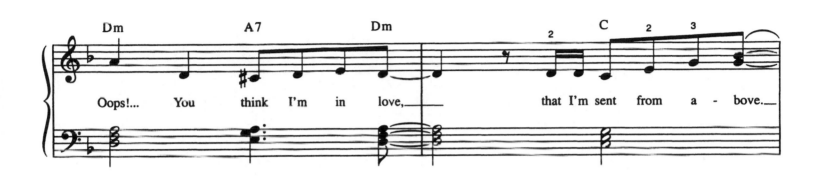

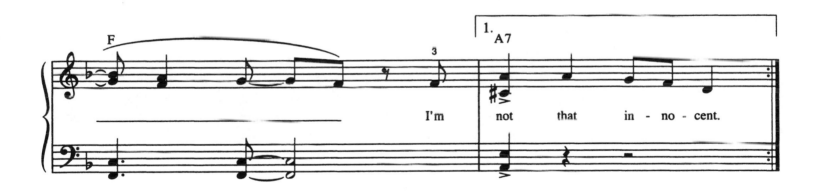

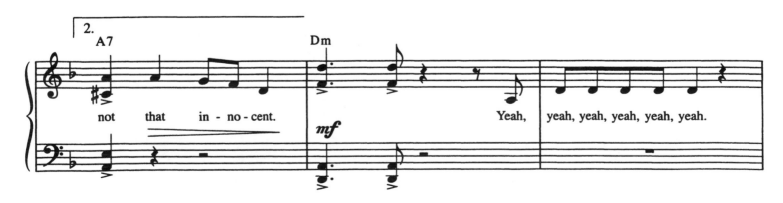

Yeah, yeah, yeah, yeah, yeah, yeah.

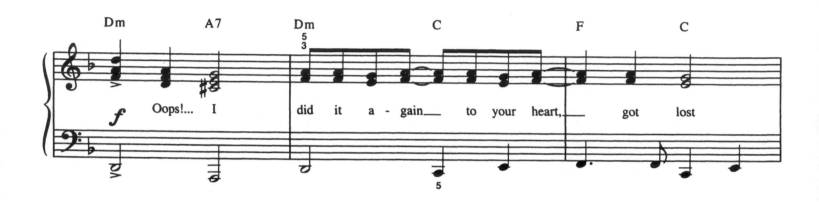

Oops!... I did it a-gain___ to your heart,___ got lost

in this game, oh, ba - by.___ Oops!... You think that I'm sent___ from a - bove.___

___ I'm not that in - no - cent.

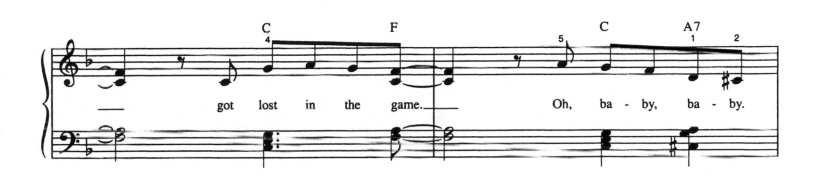

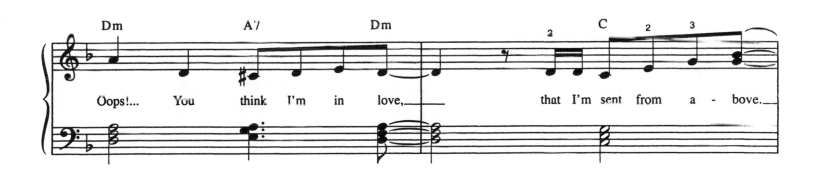

# SHAPE OF MY HEART

Words and Music by
MAX MARTIN, RAMI
and LISA MISKOVSKY
*Arranged by DAN COATES*

© 2000 Zomba Music Publishing Ltd. and Universal Music Publishing Scandinavia AB
All Rights on behalf of Zomba Music Publishing Ltd. Administered by Zomba Enterprises Inc. for U. S. and Canada
All Rights for Universal Music Publishing Scandinavia AB Administered in the Western Hemisphere by Universal Music Corp
All Rights Reserved

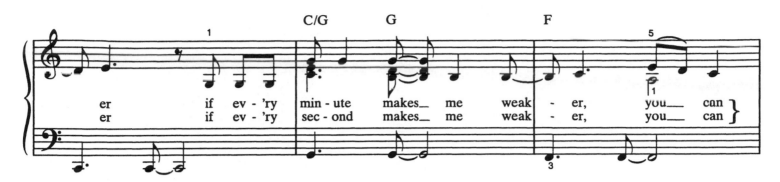

**Chorus:**

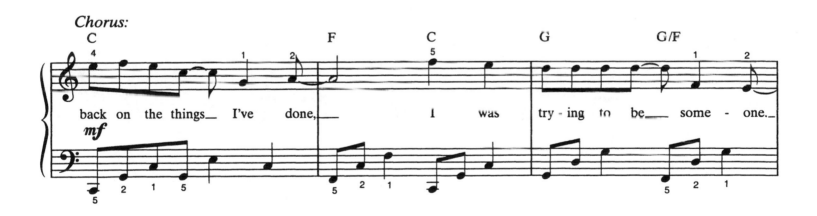

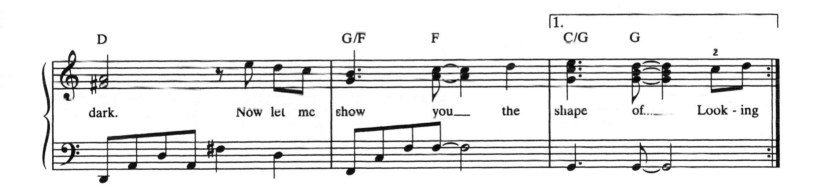

Shape of My Heart - 4 - 4

# STRONGER

Words and Music by
MAX MARTIN and RAMI
*Arranged by DAN COATES*

**Moderately, with a strong beat (♩= 108)**

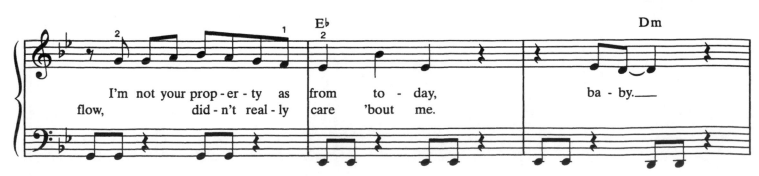

Stronger - 4 - 1

© 2000 ZOMBA MUSIC PUBLISHERS LTD.
All Rights Administered by ZOMBA ENTERPRISES INC. for the U. S. and Canada
All Rights Reserved

Oh, yeah.___ Here I go, on my own. I don't

need no - bod - y, bet - ter off a - lone. Here I go,_ on my own now.

I don't need no - bod - y, not an - y - bod - y.

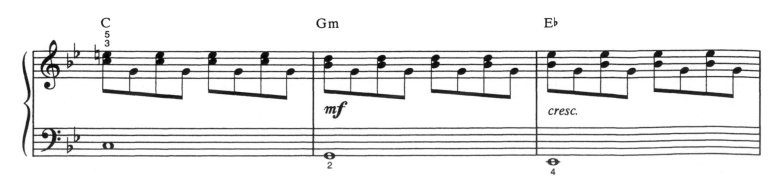

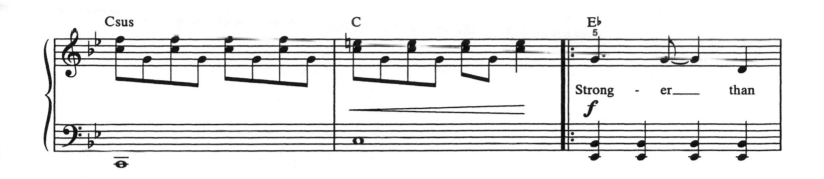

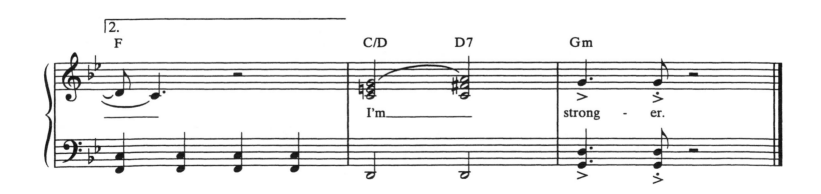

Stronger - 4 - 4

# BREAKAWAY

Words and Music by
MATTHEW GERRARD, AVRIL LAVIGNE
and BRIDGET BENENATE
*Arranged by DAN COATES*

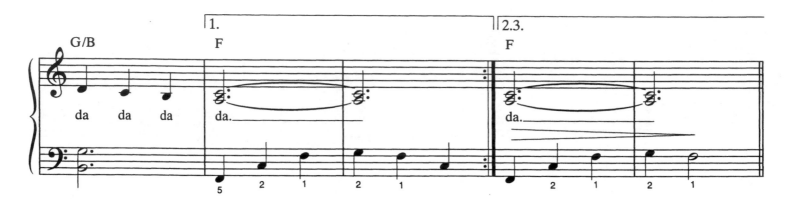

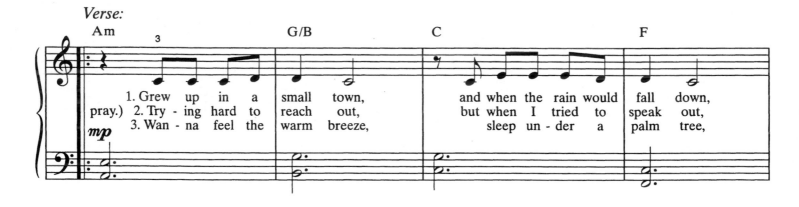

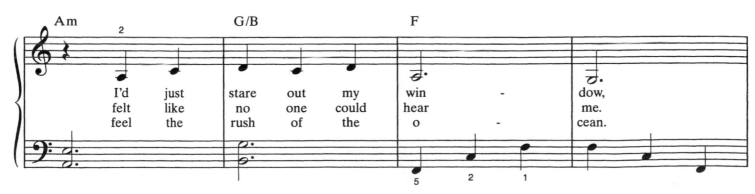

© 2004 WB Music Corp., G Matt Music, Almo Music Corp., Avril Lavigne Publishing Ltd.,
Music of Windswept, Blotter Music and Friends Of Seagulls Music
All Rights for G Matt Music Administered by WB Music Corp.
All Rights for Avril Lavigne Publishing Ltd. Administered by Almo Music Corp.
All Rights Reserved

# THIS I PROMISE YOU

Words and Music by
**RICHARD MARX**
*Arranged by DAN COATES*

**Slowly (♩ = 84)**

*(with pedal)*

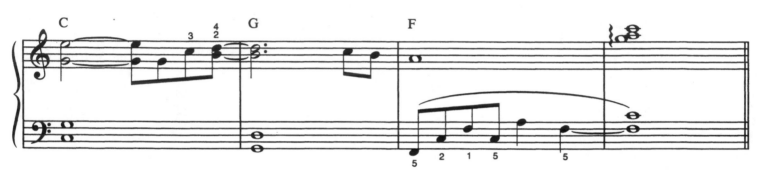

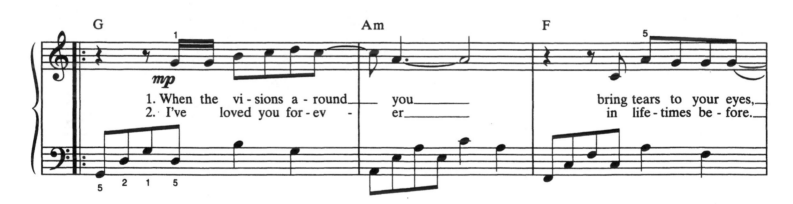

1. When the vi-sions a-round you bring tears to your eyes,
2. I've loved you for-ev-er in life-times be-fore.

and all that sur-rounds you
And I prom-ise you, nev - er

This I Promise You - 4 - 1

© 2000 CHI-BOY MUSIC
All Rights outside the U.S. and Canada for CHI-BOY MUSIC Administered by WB MUSIC CORP.
All Rights Reserved

94

# SHOW ME THE MEANING OF BEING LONELY

Words and Music by
MAX MARTIN and HERBERT CRICHLOW
*Arranged by DAN COATES*

**Moderately slow**

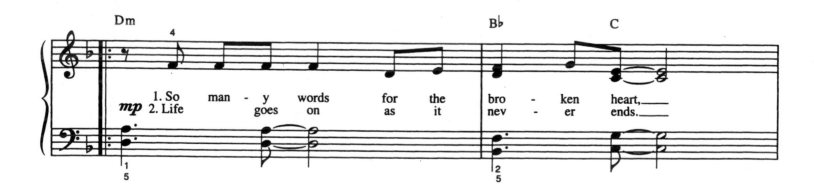

1. So man - y words for the bro - ken heart,____
2. Life goes on as it nev - er ends.____

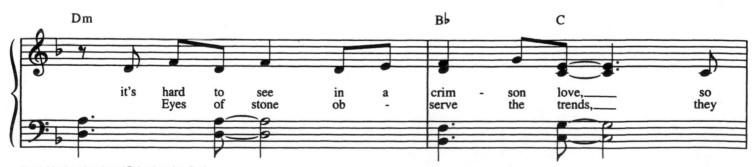

it's hard to see in a crim - son love,____ so
Eyes of stone ob - serve the trends,____ they

Show Me the Meaning of Being Lonely - 5 - 1

© 1999 GRANTSVILLE PUBLISHING LTD./MEGASONG PUBLISHING APS
(All Rights on behalf of GRANTSVILLE PUBLISHING LTD. Administered by ZOMBA ENTERPRISES INC for the U.S.A. and Canada)
All Rights Reserved

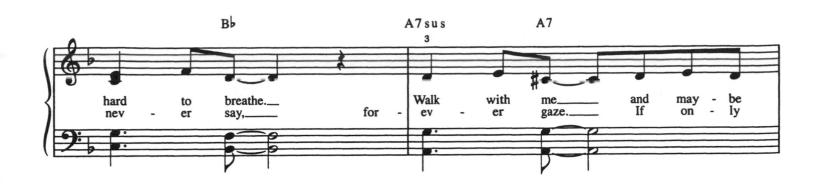

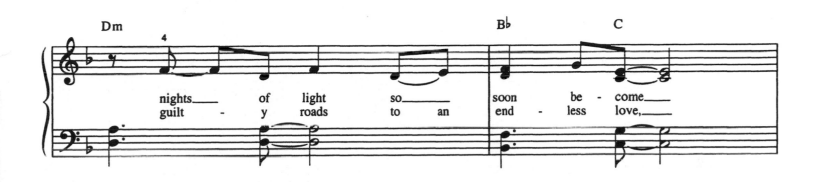

heart. There's no - where to run, I have no place to go.

Sur - ren - der my heart, bod - y and soul.

How can it be you're ask - ing me to feel the things you nev - er

show? Tell me why I can't be there where you are.

the Meaning of Being Lonely - 5 - 4